THE GREAT INDIAN PILGRIMAGE TOURISM

DR ANSHUMALI PANDEY

Made with ♥ on the Notion Press Platform
www.notionpress.com

Contents

Preface

In this book we have discussed important pilgrimage and religious centers of India in terms of their importance and studies tourist aspects related to them. The book focuses upon the ancient concept of the pilgrimage and the changing scenario of pilgrimage tourism. Our forefathers had tremendous sense of physical landscapes. They searched beautiful sights for the purpose of pilgrimage. Gradually, the ancient concepts of getting solace and peace through hardships, but people are now looking for luxuries, pleasure and comforts on their pilgrimage tour. This very need for 'comforts' itself changed the overall concept of pilgrimage tourism. This has led to the development of 'tertiary' sector in these areas and has venture in the rise of towns as well as various crafts. There are some pilgrims centers which are area specific but pilgrimage tourism, on account of the location of various centers, has sufficient space and potential to combine pleasure with piety.

Dr Anshumali Pandey

CHAPTER ONE

The Great Indian Pilgrimage Tourism

The evolution of tourism is attributed to journeys undertaken since ancient times to places considered as sacred. In common parlance, visitation to sacred places is considered pilgrimage or tirtha-yatra. Tirtha-Yatra not only means physically visiting the holy places but also implies mental and moral discipline.

People travelled solo or in groups for the purpose of spiritual or to attain salvation or moksha. In India, since time immemorial, tourism has been associated with places of religious significance. These destinations are scattered all over the country. Every religion has its sacred foci to which man of faith periodically converge. From the most ancient civilization to the present times, sacred centers have exerted a powerful pull factor of believers. The Sumerians of antiquity, who reverently ascended the step of the Ziggurat to reach the gate of heaven, have their modern counterpart in the devout Jews and Christians who visit the holy land and in the multitude of Muslims from diverse parts of the world who undertake the Hajj Yatra to Mecca.

The present unit focuses upon the ancient concept of the pilgrimage (tirthatan). In ancient time the tirth-yatras were related with 'geopiety' but in present time, the concept of pilgrimage has purely changing. Today, most of pilgrimage tourists want luxuries, pleasure and comforts on their pilgrimage tour.

In this book we also take up some case studies of pilgrimage centers in India. So you will find how pilgrimage tourism is fast developing in India and holds tremendous potential for domestic tourists.

Concept and Importance of Pilgrimage:

Man at a very early stage learnt to survive by keeping constantly on the move from one pasturing group to another, exhausting each in turn. Perhaps, traces of nomadic urge exist in all of us. But the first travelers were traders, and tourism as a pleasurable activity began with flamboyant Romans. (Bridges, J.B., 1956). In India, however, it all began with pilgrims and pilgrimages. The institution of pilgrimages has its source in our Indian civilization, though the tirtha – concept of religious tourism was quite comprehensive, it nevertheless, symbolized the twin spirit of religion and tourism.

In its broadest sense, "Pilgrimage was travelling for Wanderlust" (Shankratayan, Rahul, 1959). Wish fulfillment was an important factor. People tried to find solace and solutions to their problems in supernatural powers. Belief is important. Teerth Yatras were undertaken so every religion has its sacred foci to which man of faith periodically converge. From the most ancient civilization to the present times, sacred centers have exerted a powerful pull on the believers. Religions like Islam is also associated with it "Ajmer Sharif Urs" and visit to Nizzamuddin Dargah are example of it. Pilgrims in India visited shrines, rivers, mountains and springs. This practice can be seen even today in different religions in India. Routes used by merchants were followed. Monasteries provided refreshments and rest to the pilgrims. Even today this class of tourism constitutes a major portion. People travel to gain 'Punya'.

The nature of Hindu pilgrimage is capsule in the Indian expression tirtha-yatra. In common parlance, visitation to sacred places is considered tirtha-yatra. Basically tirtha-yatra is a journey, undertaken for the sake of worship and/ or to pay respect to a site of special religious significance. The origin and evolution of the tirtha-yatra tradition of Hindus seems to be as old as their civilization or perhaps even older than that. The practice of pilgrimage in Hinduism follows from some of the basic underpinnings of its philosophy.

Four dominant ideas have persisted in Hindu thought concerning attitudes to life. These are dharma, artha, kama and moksha. Dharma is characterized by "considerations of righteousness, duty and virtue", Artha entails material gain, worldly advantage and success. Kama signifies love and pleasure. The fourth, moksha is the spiritual realization and self-emancipation which has been equated by some scholars with salvation or freedom from transmigration. Journey to sacred places provides opportunity for the householder to detach himself for some time the cares and worries of daily life and to devote that time to prayer, contemplation, and listening to the spiritual discourses of holy men.

History of pilgrimage tourism in India, its origin, growth and development, is closely associated with our ancient development. Every mountain, peak, river and kunda is held sacred in India. Historically India has a long and prestigious background well documented in the Pauranic literature. The land is closely associated with legendary heroes of the Ramayana and Mahabharat epics who have left their imprint in the names of many places, the devotional lives of the people and even on social customs and cultural activities.

The great Adiguru Shankaracharya from South India (Kerala) trekked to India in the 8th century AD and established Badrinath, Dwarika, Jagarnath Puri and Rameshwarm as the four dham to revive Hinduism. There are so many temples in the different part of India dedicated to different Hindu deities and other religion.

Most sacred among them are the 'Panch Badris', 'Panch Kedars', 'Panch Prayags', 'Hemkund Sahib', 'Meenakshi Temple', 'Chari Sharif', 'Golden Temple', 'Haridwar' 'Kamakhya Temple' and 'Sirdi Temple' etc. While Badrinath, Kedarnath, Gangotri, Yamuotri, Hemkund, Amarnath and Vaisno Devi etc. are centres of national significance, others are a number of pilgrim centres which may more appropriately be called satellites or adjuncts to the major pilgrim centers.

Tourism and Pilgrimage:

Tourism and Pilgrimage are closely related. Pilgrimage tourism helps greatly in promotion of the destination.

Earlier, pilgrimage was associated with 'purity of thought' and undertaken for expiation of sins or for salvation. The concept of the pilgrimage was, 'the harder the journey the better the reward.' Thus, the pilgrimage needed minimum infrastructural facilities. But in present time, pilgrimage is pleasure-oriented and demands vast infrastructure in the tertiary sector. Thus, the meet the ever increasing demand for better travel facilities for the number of pilgrim tourists at pilgrim centers the state government and tourism department develop infrastructure and provide various facilities and amenities for the visitors. Chardham Yatra in this region can be sited as an example. The journey in the past was quite tedious and hazardous. Recently, however, the roads have got totally rebuilt, and the transport is easily available. Today there places are well connected by motor vehicle. Many pilgrim centers which were earlier small town, but on their religious importance have now emerged as big city. For example Shirdi, a very small village, now on account of the increasing popularity of Shirdi Saint's shrine is fast developing into a big town with a number of hotels coming up. Similarly Katra in Jammu a small town, now has a no of hotels with various types of facilities available here. Religious centers also develop into good shopping spots for traditional local handicrafts, paintings and food items. So large numbers of devotees travelling to religious centers generate handsome revenue and are the source of livelihood to local people who depend on the tourist's inflow.

Potential of Pilgrimage Tourism:

The scope of pilgrimage tourism can be called area specific because if one is the devotee of a particular religion, visit repetitively those religious centers where his worshipping deity resides. After sometime, he may lose his interest, owing to lack of any other adventure and tourism activities. In spite of this limited scope, pilgrimage tourism has enough potential to develop domestic tourism. If we analyses the traditional pilgrim centers which are associated with rivers, their confluences, coasts or hill area. Our forefathers had tremendous sense of physical landscapes.

They searched beautiful sights for the purpose of pilgrimage. They have associated pilgrim with 'geo piety'. Tirthatan provided them opportunity to break away from the cares and worries of the mundane world. The locations of the traditional pilgrim centers are such that it can always serve dual purpose of pilgrimage and adventure. If you goes to Gangotri will certainly excite your urge to go for trekking. Similarly, while landing at Nainital can you restrict your visit to Nainital Lake only! Will the charm of Jim Corbett National Park not lure you? This clearly indicates that one can not restrict pilgrimage tourism to specific area boundaries. It has tremendous potential to develop tourism and provide other tourism activities with various facilities for the tourist in around the pilgrimage centre.

Changing Patterns of Pilgrimage Tourism:

Change is an eternal process - essentially germane to all the manifestations of the nature - 'animate to inanimate' and 'structures to functions'. It is owing to this process that life evolved and diversified on the planet earth. It led to the origin of mankind and its present day prosperity which is progressively moving ahead. Ecologists and bio and geoscientists use the term 'succession' to explain as to how any why a densely forested area transforms in to a desert and vice versa, or, why and how a species consistently changes itself with the dynamically changing environment or, dies-out to give way to another species better suited to the prevailing environmental conditions.

Obviously, pilgrimages as a concept, tradition, ritual, value, system or philosophy too has not been and would never be beyond nature's indispensable scheme of change. Immerged as the earliest for of organized travel. Thus, in all parts of the world and in case of all the religions, the legacy of pilgrimages, over the time, has consistently witnessed changes in many ways. What-ever one's objective of practicing 'pilgrimage', it has paramount significance from both 'individual' and 'societal' perspectives because:

(i) It engages all human capabilities (audio-visual, motor, emotional);

(ii) It highlights and deepens the mutual bonds that are a very important factor in religious emotions;

(iii) It stresses the value and prolongs remembrance of the religious events that are connected with the place,

(iv) It strengthens the socio-economical, cultural, spiritual and civilizing bonds that surpass the boundaries of a race or even a nation.

In the process of travel and sojourn, the pilgrims interact, learn, sell, buy, exchange material and spiritual goods en-route and at the destination, get acquainted with the socio-cultural values of the hosts amidst whom they come as strangers but go back while leaving behind strong social bonds.

As observed in the fore-going, pilgrimage has been an age-old practice in all parts of the world, and more so in India where religion has been intricately linked with 'essence of life'. Thus, in all the sects of Hinduism, the concept of pilgrimage is keenly guided by the philosophy of Dharma (ethics/duties), Samsara (the continuing cycle of birth, life, death and rebirth), Karma (action and subsequent reaction), Moksha (liberation from samsara) and the various Yogas (paths or practices). Hindu practices generally involve seeking awareness of God and sometimes also seeking blessings from Devas. Therefore, Hinduism has developed numerous practices meant to help the people to think of divinity in the midst of everyday life.

Hindus can engage in puja (worship or veneration) either at home or at a temple. At home, they often create a shrine with icons dedicated to the individual's chosen form(s) of God. Temples are usually dedicated to a primary deity along with associated subordinate deities. Visiting temples is not obligatory. In fact, many visit temples only during religious festivals. Worship is performed through icons (murtis). The icons serve as a tangible link between the worshiper and God. The image is often considered as the manifestation of God, since God is imminent. The Padma Purana states that 'the murti is not to be thought of as mere stone or wood but as a manifest form of the Divinity'. In fact, the Hinduism has a developed system of symbolism and iconography to represent the sacred in art, architecture, literature and worship. These symbols gain their meaning from the scriptures, mythology, or cultural traditions.

The syllable Om (which represents the Parabrahman) and the Swastika sign (which symbolizes auspiciousness) have grown to represent Hinduism itself, while other markings such as tilaka identify a follower of the faith. Hinduism associates many symbols, which include the lotus, chakra and veena, with particular deities. Mantras are invocations, praise and prayers. Their meaning, sound, and chanting style enable a devotee to focus on holy thoughts or express devotion to God/the deities. Many devotees perform morning ablutions at the bank of a sacred river while chanting the Gayatri Mantra or Mahamrityunjaya Mantras. The epic Mahabharata extols Japa (ritualistic chanting) as the greatest duty in the Kali Yuga (what Hindus believe to be the current age). True to this, Japa is a common spiritual practice among the Hindus in particular. Going by the religious dictum, one must regularly and religiously perform pooja with Mantras and Japa in the prescribed manner, at home or in a close by shrine, and should also essentially visit the teerthas.

The word Teertha is derived from the Sanskrit root 'tri' which means to be free; by adding 'th' its meaning becomes the one who frees you from the world. According to this explanation, synonyms for Teerthas are gods, holy places, scriptures, gurus and sacred Karmas, as all of them are the source of attaining spiritual purity, enlightenment, prosperity or moksha depending on the way one takes it. Expectedly, over the years, the number and types of pilgrims visiting the holy shrines, as also their motivation /demand / expectation / satisfaction / behavior patterns, have consistently changed in accordance to the change socio-cultural, economic and ecological changed incurring in their on environment, as well as, in the environment of the destination region. The dynamic advancements in the technological sphere followed by the urbanization and modernization processes are obviously the factors responsible, to this effect. Owing to ever improving accessibility facility, now it is easier to visit the otherwise distant destinations.

Effective means of communication make it even handier. Consistently increasing disposable income and discretionary time (Leisure) available to more and more people, on the other hand, is making it possible to more and more people to go on pilgrimages, even those who could not have otherwise been able to travel owing to their physical limitations. The steadily enhancing awareness level is creating more and more reasons to travel religious destinations than traveling exclusively for pilgrimages. Thus, not so devout people are also traveling out of the zeal to see the Himalayan grandeur or the colorful cultural spectrum of the region, alongside having the darshana of the deity.

Consequently, the demographic pattern of the pilgrims is also changing in terms of age, sex, occupation and income levels its. It is no more confined to the elderly pilgrims; rather people from almost all age groups are now traveling to the shrine resorts. Demand patterns of the pilgrims to is consistently changing in accordance to their changing life style vis a vis provision of diverse facilities at and en-route the pilgrim centers.

CHAPTER TWO

Important Hindu Religious Centers

The various religious centers of the god and goddesses dotting the different part of India, represent the abiding faith of the Indian people in them, the reverence with which they look up to them, and the obeisance they pay in the temples constructed in their names. There are temples of representing 'divine knowledge', Durga Mata, the 'Fire' from of Lord Shiva and 'Chandika' Kali Mata. So we can divided Indian religious centers into two main categories: Firstly, the certain religious centers which are already established for pilgrimage from ancient times, e.g. Gangotri, Yamunotri, Kedarnath, Badrinath and Mata Vaishno Devi etc. and Second type of religious centres are those which on account of their geopolitical situation and availability of space and other amenities facilitated the development of a religious centre. These religious centers are scattered all over the India. Some prominent religious centre is listed below:

- **Northern India:** Banaras, Badrinath, Kedarnath, Gangotri, Yamunotri, Vaishno Devi, Haridwar, Ayodhya, Chari Sharif, Amarnath, Chitrakut and Hemkund etc.
- **Eastern India:** Jagannath Puri Temple, Konark Temple, Bodh Gaya, Kamakhya Devi Temple, Belur Math and Kali Ghat Temple etc.
- **Western India:** Dilwara, Dwarika, Somnath, Ajmer, Ujjain, Junagarh, Shirdi and Pushkar Temple etc.
- **Southern India:** Rameshwaram, Aurobindo Ashram, Kanyakumari, Meenakshi Temple and Madurai Temple etc.

Banaras (Varanasi)

Banaras - Varanasi - Kaasi is considered to be the holiest of all pilgrimage sites in India. Banaras in Uttar Pradesh is amongst the oldest living cities in the world. Banaras is located between two rivers Varana and Asi, and hence the name Varanasi. Thousands of pilgrims come to Banaras daily to take a ritual dip in the sacred river Ganga, as it is believed that it will cleanse their souls of sins, and to worship God at its many temples. Banaras houses the Kaasi Visweswara (Visanatha) temple, enshrining one of the twelve Jyotirlingams of Lord Shiva. It is so old that it is a part of Indian mythology and finds mention in the epics Ramayana and Mahabharata. It has nearly hundred ghats. Many are bathing ghats but at the others, cremations are conducted. According to Hindu belief, dying at Kashi (Banaras) ensures release from the eternal cycle of birth and rebirth.

Haridwar

Haridwar which is also known as the gateway of the Gods is another important city with religious importance.

Haridwar stands as the gateway to the four pilgrimages of Uttarakhand also known as the Char Dhams of Uttarakhand– Gangotri, Yamunotri, Kedarnath and Badrinath. The follower of Lord Shiva (Har) and follower of Lord Vishnu (Hari) pronounce this place Hardwar and Haridwar respectively. Haridwar has been sanctified by the presence of three Gods; Brahma, Vishnu and Mahesh. Lord Vishnu is said to have his footprints on a stone that is set in the upper wall of Har-ki-Pauri where the holy Ganga toughes it all the times. Devout believers feel that they can go to heaven by getting their salvation after a dip in the sacred Ganga at Haridwar. Two great events that take place here are the memorable Kumbh Mela, which happens once every twelve years and the Ardh Kumbh Mela, which comes once every six years.

Mata Vaishno Devi

A pilgrimage to the holy shrine of Mata Vaishno Devi is considered to be one of the holiest pilgrimages of our times. Popular the world over as 'Manh Maangi Muradein Poori Karne Wali Mata', which means, the Mother who fulfils whatever her children wish for, Shri Mata Vaishno Devi resides in a holy cave located in the folds of the three peaked mountain named Trikuta (pronounced as Trikoot). The Holy cave attracts lakhs of devotees every year. In fact, the number of yatris visiting the holy shrine annually now exceeds 5 million. This is due to the unflinching faith of the devotees who throng the shrine from all parts of India and abroad.

Ujjain

Ujjain, a historic capital of Central India in Madhya Pradesh is a venerated pilgrimage center enshrining Mahakaleshwara, one of the Jyotirlinga manifestations of Lord Shiva. The Mahakaleshwar temple is located near a lake. It has five levels, one of which is underground. Also in Ujjain is the temple to Parvati-Harasiddhi Devi temple.

Panch Prayags

Prayag means confluene of two or more rivers. These prayags are termed holy in religious epics like Ramayana and Mahabharata. From Centuries, people take holy bath in these Prayags. It is said that the water of Holy River is supposed to washaway the sins. There are five Prayags in Uttarakhand known as Vishnu Prayag, Dev Prayag, Rudra Prayag, Karan Prayag and Nand Prayag. These are collectively called the Panch Prayags.

Important Pilgrimage Centre

Four Dhamas (India Level):

'Dham' means "Abode of God". The great 8th century reformer and philosopher Adi Guru Shankaracharya was prominently involved in reviving the Hindu Dharma in India. He travelled throughout the country and grouped the four sacred places Badrinath, Jagannath Puri, Dwarka and Rameshwaram, as the Char Dham. At three of the Dhams Lord Vishnu and His Avatar Lord Krishna are worshipped while at one Dham, Rameshwaram, Lord Shiva is the resident deity. All of four dhams at the four corners of India symbolize the essential unity of India's spiritual traditions and values. In the north is Badrinath, to the east is puri, to the west Dwarka and to the south Rameshwaram. Each of the four dhams is a citadel of ancient temples and religious monuments, with on most significant temple as its distinguishing landmark. To the Hindu the land of his or her forefathers is benignly watched over at all times by the gracious protector of all – Lord Vishnu – preserver and extenuator - and Lord Shiva - the forgetful benefactor - lost in fumes of cannabis but benign as ever. As with Muslims, who aspire to visit the holy city of Mecca at least once in a lifetime, the Hindu aspires to visit all four Dhams at least once in a lifetime. This is the most blessed of all pilgrimages assuring freedom from sins and ensuring Moksha – salvation from the miserable cycle of life and death.

A. Badrinath:

Badrinath or the ***Badrivishal***, one of the four *Hindu Dhamas*, is the most prominent shrine resort in district Chamoli (Garhwal Region) of the State of Uttarakhand dating back to Vedic times. Dedicated to Lord Vishnu, the shrine is believed to be reinstated by Adi Shankaracharya, who also established a 'Math' (Joshimath), about 48 km downstream from Badrinath which serves as winter seat of the Lord. On account of being situated in the Greater Himalayan Zone, the shrine resort has spectacularly fascinating natural grandeur all around with inherently spiritual ambience.

Badri refers to a berry that was said to grow abundantly in the area, and nath means Lord. The legend goes that in the 8th century AD Adi Shankaracharya discovered a black stone image of Lord Badrinarayan made of Saligram stone from the Narad Kund and consecrated it in a cave near Tapt Kund hot springs. In the sixteenth century, the King of Garhwal moved the murti to the present temple. The sacred township is settled at the height of 3110 mt. above the sea level along the either banks of the turbulent Alaknanda River that flows southwards, embracing the Rishi Ganga to the south of Badrinath.

Geographically speaking, this holy resort runs longitudinally between the coordinates 30°44'56" North and 79°31'20" East, into a spacious 4.5 km. long and 1.5 km. wide valley that opens-up northwards to the *Bhotiya* village of *Mana - the last settlement along the Alaknanda Valley.* Badrinath valley is flanked by the *Nar and Narayana* Mountains with the awe-inspiringly beautiful peak of Nilkantha on the backdrop. Interestingly, the *Nar Parvat* is also called as *Kuber Bhandar* (treasury of the Lord of Wealth), after the popular belief for containing diamonds and emeralds.

The Badri Vishal Temple standing about 15 mt high on the right banks of the Alaknanda River has a gushing hot water spring *(Tapta Kunda)* close to it. The pilgrims take a holy dip in the Tapt Kund before entering the temple.

There are a number of important places and sites of religious significance in and around Badrinath, like *Tapta Kund, Narad Kund, Panch Shilas, Panch Dharas, Brahma Kapal, Charanpaduka, Sesha Netra, Nilkanth Peak, Urvasi Temple, Mata Murti, Bhim Pul and, Vasudhara Falls, Satopanth* and *Swargarohini* further upstream. The temple remains closed from October to April due to the winter snow, when temperatures fall to sub-zero degrees.

B. Jagannath Puri

Jagannath Puri located in the Eastern Indian state of Orissa. Jagannath Puri is one of the oldest cities in the eastern part of the country. It is situated on the coast of the Bay of Bengal. The resident Deity at the main temple is Lord Jagannath (Lord of the Universe). He is present together with His elder brother Balaram, who is believed to be an avatar of Shesha, the snake on whom Vishnu usually rests, and His younger sister Subhadra, who may be an incarnation of Lakshmi. Lord Jagannath is unmarried here and is closely associated with Krishna, Vishnu's eighth avatar.

The main temple here is about 1000 years old and constructed by Raja Choda Ganga Deva and Raja Tritiya Ananga Bhima Deva. Puri is the site of the Govardhana Matha, one of the four cardinal institutions or Mathas established by Adi Guru Shankaracharya. The Puri temple is one of the holiest shrines in India and it is regularly visited by millions of devotees every year. The unique feature of the Puri Jagannath Temple is the Ratha Yatra. A ratha is a chariot and these chariots are really big.

C. Dwarka Puri

Dwarka is as old as the history of India. It is located in the Western Indian state of Gujrat. The city derives its name from word dvar meaning door or gate. It is located close to where the Gomti River merges into the Gulf of Kutch. The city lies in the westernmost part of India. It was the seat of Sri Krishna after He quit Mathura, His maternal home, to come and reign here. Since it has been held as holy for a long time it has gradually accumulated, over the years, a large number of religious monuments and institutions that today make it one of the most revered spots in Hinduism.

Adi Shankaracharya, one of the most learned and sanctified personalities in Hinduism, built one of his four maths here. It is still an institution where Hindu scriptures are studied and their inherent meanings deciphered. The main Dham temple houses Ranchchodji, another name for Lord Krishna who time and often fled from the battlefield under unfavorable circumstances to return again another day and win. “Ran” means “War” while “Chod” means “Running away”.

There is also a temple to Lord Krishna’s wife Rukmini, who is believed to be an incarnation of Lakshmi, the goddess of wealth and beauty. This small temple is an architectural masterpiece. The temple walls are decorated with beautiful paintings depicting Rukmini's pastimes with Lord Krishna. This temple is dating back to the 12th century. Also resident near Dwarka is the Jyotirlinga temple of Nageshwar. Dwarka is so entwined with legends and myths that the pilgrim is overcome with religious fervor upon setting foot on its sacred soil.

D. Rameshwaram

Rameshwaram is the only one of the four Dhams where the resident Deity is Lord Shiva. Rameswaram located in the Southern Indian state of Tamil Nadu. It is situated in the Gulf of Mannar at the very tip of the Indian peninsula. According to legends, this is the place from where Lord Rama, Vishnu's seventh avatar, worshipped Shiva prior to His attack on Lankapuri, the capital city of the Rakshasas to rescue his beloved wife Sita who had been abducted by Ravana, king of the Rakshasas..

The Ramanatha Swamy Temple dedicated to Lord Shiva occupies a major area of Rameshwaram. Rameshwaram is significant for the Hindus as a pilgrimage to Banaras is incomplete without a pilgrimage to Rameswaram. The presiding deity here is in the form of a Linga with the name Sri Ramanatha Swamy, it also is one of the twelve Jyotirlingas. Sethu Karai is a place 22 km before the island of Rameshwaram from where God Ram built a Floating Stone Bridge "Ramasethu" till Rameshwaram that further continued from Dhanushkodi in Rameshwaram till Talaimannar in Sri Lanka as mentioned in the great Hindu epic Ramayana. The ruins of the Ramasethu are submerged under the sea as shot from Gemini 1 satellite of NASA in 2004.

Four Dhamas (Uttarakhand State):

Pilgrimage has a long tradition in Hinduism. The origins of the Char Dham remain obscure. The appellation Char Dham had been reserved for India's most famous pilgrimage circuit, four important temples—Puri, Rameshwaram, Dwarka, and Badrinath. They had been grouped together by the great eighth-century reformer and philosopher Shankaracharya (Adi Guru Sankara) as the archetypal All-India pilgrimage circuit to the four cardinal points of the subcontinent.

Badrinath, the last visited and the most important of the four sites in the original Char Dham, also became the cornerstone site of a Himalayan pilgrimage circuit dubbed the Chota (little) Char Dham. Unlike the original Char Dham, the sites of the Chota Char Dham have their own, separate sectarian affiliation. The three major sectarian movements in modern devotional Hinduism have representation, with the Vaishnava site Badrinath joined by one Shaiva site (Kedarnath) and two Devi sites (Yamunotri and Gangotri). Each site has its own unique characteristics. As late as the mid-twentieth century, devotees consistently still used the "Chota" designation to designate the Himalayan version of the Char Dham. That usage reflects the importance of the circuit for most of its history.

All four pilgrimage sites sit in the Himalayas, previously difficult to reach, requiring a two month hike. During that time, only wandering ascetics, Hindu masters, and wealthy devotees with an entourage made the pilgrimage. Since the Sino-Indian War of 1962, when India made road improvements in the region to conduct campaigns against China, travel to the sites has become easier for pilgrims.Currently, the Char Dham sees upwards of

250,000 visitors in an average pilgrimage season, which lasts from approximately April 15 until Diwali (sometime in November). The pilgrimage season has the heaviest traffic in the two-month period before the monsoon. Despite the danger, pilgrims continue to visit the Char Dham in the monsoon period, as well as after the rains end. Although temperatures at the shrines in the early winter months (October and November) prove inhospitable, the incredible mountain scenery that surrounds the sites has the most vividness after the rains have moistened the dust of the plains below.

Most pilgrims to the Char Dham embark from the famous temple town of Haridwar. Others leave from Haridwar's sister city, Rishikesh, or from Dehra Dun, the capital of Uttarakhand. From there, pilgrims traditionally visit the Char Dham Yatra in the following order:

A. Yamunotri

Yamunotri (3323 mt.), as evident from the name it self, the place is related to the origin of the second most sacred river of the country, *viz., the Yamuna.* In the traditions of Char Dham Yatra of Uttarakhand, this western most shrine is to be visited first. Perched atop a flank of the Bandarpunch Peak, this religious centre is in fact situated opposite the Gangotri Dhama. Yamunotri River originates from the Champasar Glacier lying one km ahead of where Yamunotri Shrine is presently located. Surya Kund and Divya Shila are two of the more important religious sites located in close vicinity of the temple.

Near the temple is the hot water pool known as Jamunabai Kund. A dip in the kund is most rejuvenating and refreshing. The pandas of Yamunotri come from the village of Kharsali, which is on the other bank of the Yamuna near Jankibaichatti. The Temple opens each year on the auspicious day of Akshaya-Tritiya, which generally falls during the last week of April, or the first week of May. The Temple always closes on the sacred day of Diwali with a brief ceremony.

B. Gangotri

The importance of ***Gangotri*** (3140 m) area is quite evident from the fact that it is associated with the origin of the holy mother Ganga, originating from the Gangotri *(Ganga descended)*. The present day Gangotri located in the midst of giant deodars and conifers seems to have been once the site of the snout of the Gangotri which owing to the obvious geo-physical processes have retreated to it present location (i.e., the present day Gaumukh). Presence of the Bhagirath Shila (where the legendary king is believed to have meditated to get the Ganga to the earth from the heaven) close to the Gangotri Temple support this view.

The present ***Gangotri Temple***, a white marvel of architecture, is said to have been constructed by the Gorkha Chieftain Amar Singh centuries back. People from all parts of country, and the Hindu settlements world over, have undying faith in these shire. The pujaris are Brahmins from the village of Mukhwa. Like Yamunotri, the shrine of Gangotri opens each year on the auspicious day of Akshaya-Tritiya, which generally falls during the last week of April, or the first week of May. The Temple always closes on the sacred day of Diwali with a brief ceremony.

C. Kedarnath

The main shrine, the Kedarnath - one of the '*Twelve Jyotirlingas*' is located at 30˚44'15" latitude and 79˚68'33" longitude at an altitude of 3583 mt. on the foothills of the beautiful Manapath mountain. Kedarnath is approachable on foot through 14 km long trek from Gaurikund which in-turn is connected by road with Rishikesh, Dehradun,

Kotdwara and other places of Uttarakhand.

The temple of Kedarnath is a unique marvel of architecture. There are a number of 'Kunds' in the vicinity of Kedarnath, i.e., Peeth. Shiv Kund, Udak Kund, Rudhir Kund, Hans Kund etc. while the huge *Gandhi Sarovar* or the *Chorawari Tal* is located on the backdrop of the main shrine. In fact, as per the legend, when Pandavas were following Lord Shiva to please him so that they could get rid of the sin of the Brahmhatya (*sin of killing the Brahmins* or the *Gurus*) and *Kul Hatya* (killing the members of own clan), found him at present Kedarnath. The Lord did not want to meet him and hence is said to have transformed into a buffalo and got mixed with the herd of buffaloes grazing there. When identified by Bhima, the Lord in the form of buffalo began to sink.

Since Bhima could catch hold of only the hump part, it remained at Kedarnath while the remaining body parts appeared at four different places, i.e., face at Rudranath, belly at Madhyamaheshwar, shoulders at Tungnath, and hairs at Kalpeshwar. Thus came the 'concept of *Panch Kedars*'. Kedarnath temple opens three to four days before that of Badrinath. The opening date usually falls during the last week of April or the first week of May, and is fixed on the day of Mahashivratri by the priests of the temple at Ukhimath. The temple closes on the day after Diwali, with a brief and simple ceremony. Almost for the six months the town is snow covered and no human settlement remains there. The pandas of Kedarnath reside in the villages around Guptakashi and Ukhimath.

D. Badrinath

Badrinath or the ***Badrivishal***, one of the four *Hindu Dhamas*, is the most prominent shrine resort in district Chamoli (Garhwal Region) of the State of Uttarakhand dating back to Vedic times. Dedicated to Lord Vishnu, the shrine is believed to be reinstated by Adi Shankaracharya, who also established a 'Math' (Joshimath), about 48 km downstream from Badrinath which serves as winter seat of the Lord.

There are a number of important places and sites of religious significance in and around Badrinath, like *Tapta Kund, Narad Kund, Panch Shilas, Panch Dharas, Brahma Kapal, Charanpaduka, Sesha Netra, Nilkanth Peak, Urvasi Temple, Mata Murti, Bhim Pul and, Vasudhara Falls, Satopanth* and *Swargarohini* further upstream. Beside **Badrivishal** there are four other Badris known as ***Yogdhyan Badri, Bhavishya Badri, Vridha Badri*** and **Adi Badri**. These are collectively called the *Panch Badris* or Five Badris, respectively located at *Pandukeshwar, Tapovan, Animath and Adi Badri.*

CHAPTER THREE

KUMBHA MELA: THE WORLD'S LARGEST PILGRIMAGE GATHERING

Kumbh Mela at Prayagrag

Sacred site festivals in India (melas) are a vital part of Hindu pilgrimage traditions. Celebrating a mythological event in the life of a deity or an auspicious astrological period, melas attract enormous numbers of pilgrims from all over the country. The greatest of these, the Kumbha Mela, is a riverside festival held 4 times every 12 years, rotating between Allahabad located at the confluence of the rivers Ganga, Yamuna and the mythical Sarasvati, Nasik on the Godavari River, Ujjain on the Shipra River, and Haridvar on the Ganga.

Bathing in these rivers during the Kumbha Mela is considered an endeavor of great merit, cleansing both body and spirit. The Allahabad and Haridvar festivals are routinely attended by millions of pilgrims (13 million visited Allahabad in 1977, some 18 million in 1989, and over 28 million in 2001), making the Kumbha Mela the largest religious gathering in the world. It may also be the oldest. There are two traditions that determine the origin/ location and timing of the festival.

The origins of the location of Kumbha Mela are found in the Puranas, ancient texts that tell about a battle between gods and demons wherein four drops of amrita (nectar—drink of the gods that gives them immortality) were supposed to have fallen to earth on these mela sites (Singh and Rana 2002; Feldhaus 2003). The second tradition establishes the timeframe and is connected to astrological phenomena. The following list demonstrates the astrological periods of the four melas and the years of their most recent and near future occurrences:

> "***Allahabad*** *(Prayaga)—when Jupiter is in Aries or Taurus and the Sun and Moon are in Capricorn during the Hindu month of Magha*

(January–February): 1965, 1977, 1989, 2001, 2012, 2024.

Haridwar*—when Jupiter is in Aquarius and the Sun is in Aries during the Hindu month of Chaitra (March–April): 1962, 1974, 1986, 1998, 2010, 2021, and 2033.*

Ujjain*—when Jupiter is in Leo and the Sun is in Aries, or when Jupiter, the Sun, and the Moon are in Libra during the Hindu month of Vaishakha (April–May); 1968, 1980, 1992, 2004, 2016, 2028, 2040.*

Nasik*—when Jupiter and the Sun are in Leo in the Hindu month of Bhadrapada (August–September): 1956, 1968, 1980, 1992, 2003, 2015.*"

The antiquity of the Kumbha Mela is shrouded in mystery (Dubey 200 la, 200 1b). The Chinese Buddhist pilgrim, Hsuan-tsang, recorded a visit to Allahabad in 643 CE in the company of King Harsavardhana and described a tradition of Magha Mela; however, only around the ninth century did it take its present shape under the guidance of the great philosopher Shankaracharya, who had established four monasteries in the north, south, east and west of India, and called upon the Hindu ascetics, monks and sages to meet at these sites for an exchange of philosophical views.

Indologists speculate that between the ninth and twelfth centuries other monks and religious reformers perpetuated and reinforced this periodic assemblage of saints and laypeople at sacred places on the banks of the holy rivers to create an environment of mutual understanding among different religious sects. Additionally, the festival gave laypeople the opportunity to derive benefit from their association with the normally reclusive sages and forest yogis. What was originally a regional festival at Prayag thus became the pre-eminent pan-Indian pilgrimage gathering.

CHAPTER FOUR

Panchakroshi Yatra: Experiencing The Cosmic Circuit

The most sacred city for Hindus, Varanasi (Kashi), has a unique personality possessing all the important pan-India Hindu sacred places in abbreviated form and spatially transposed in its landscape—hence, the city's title of 'cultural capital' of India. The sacred territory (kshetra) of Kashi is delimited by a pilgrimage circuit, known as Panchakroshi.

In an abbreviated form, the Panchakroshi pilgrimage route of Varanasi symbolizes the cosmic circuit, the centre of which is the temple of Madhyameshvara and radial point at the shrine of Dehli Vinayaka, covering a distance of 88.5km. There are 108 shrines and sacred spots along this route, archetypically indicating the integrity of the division of time (e.g. 12 zodiacs) and cardinality of space (9 planets in Hindu mythology, referring to 8 directions and the centre). Among the 108 shrines, 56 are related to Shiva (lingo). The antiquity of this pilgrimage goes back to the mid-sixteenth century as described in the mythological puranas.

The commonly accepted period for this sacred journey is believed to be the intercalary (thirteenth) month of leap year, commonly known as malamasa. During the last Panchakroshi Yatra in the Ashvina Malamasa (18 September–16 October 2001), a total of 52,310 devout local pilgrims and out-of-town pilgrim-tourists performed this sacred journey. To understand pilgrim-tourist experiences better, a survey was conducted with 432 pilgrimage participants by this author during Panchakroshi Yatra.

According to the study, travel distance, level of faith, mental preparedness, cultural hierarchy, gender context, and various other life conditions, significantly influenced the intensity of the experience. The survey found that small groups (three to six persons) are the most common social setting for performing Panchakroshi Yatra, which is a finding consistent with Sopher's (1968) observations in Gujarat. The data also show the dominance of females (66.2 per cent), which supports the perception that Hindu women are 'more religious' than men.

This reflects to a large extent, the family-based nature of the pilgrimage experience. The majority of pilgrims were from a proximal area surrounding the city and district of Varanasi. In addition, people from Bengal form a significant cohort owing to the fact that Varanasi has been an important settlement destination for Bengalis since the twelfth century. The religious history of the city and the efficacy of the pilgrimage attract Hindus from all over India, and Nepal.

Likewise, in recent years there has been a notable growth in diasporic Hindus from many other countries (e.g. Singapore, United States, Canada, Fiji, South Africa, etc.) travelling to Varanasi to participate in various pilgrimages.

Well over half of the pilgrim-tourists are older people between the ages of 40 and 60. Adolescent devotees usually accompany their parents and grandparents to support and help them, but they also enjoy the fun of leisure pursuits and sightseeing in addition to the religious rituals of the pilgrimage. Approximately one-fifth of the pilgrims surveyed belong to the lower classes, including peasantry and menial servants. Where education is low and dependency on subsistence farming is high, there is a strong belief in religious and ritualistic activities.

Lower educational status is represented by a high percentage of pilgrims and vice versa. More than half (57 per cent) of the foot-pilgrims from the local region claimed to have an education between primary school and graduation (grades 5–10), while among pilgrimage-tourists it is around 70 per cent. The predominance of the Brahmin caste (the highest caste in the Hindu system) is obvious in the observance of Hindu festivals and ritual performances, for by undertaking these rituals, they rejuvenate their professional images, social position and religious status. The hierarchy of higher-lower caste has a positive correspondence with the frequency of devotees. Brahmins and Merchant castes together comprise over half of the pilgrim population.

Since India's independence in 1947 the upward mobility of the lower caste has become more notable by their adopting symbols and performing religious activities more typically associated with the higher caste. This tendency has encouraged lower caste people to take part in such sacred journeys, as set forth in Sanskrit law books and mythical anthologies. These texts explicitly designate pilgrimage as an appropriate meritorious act for poor people, members of the low caste, and women.

However, Hindus of the very lowest caste (e.g. untouchables, such as cobblers, pig-herders, sweepers, basket-makers, and mouse-eaters) almost never make pilgrimages (Morinis 1984:281). While no noticeable cultural changes have occurred in the Panchakroshi pilgrimage, socio-structural aspects have undergone important changes in the course of time.

Hindu pilgrims enjoy sacred journeys as an earthly adventure from one place to another that entails the combined effects of a spiritual quest and physical hardship—by walking, suffering or avoiding temptation. Believers often speak of the special power of pilgrimage to uplift them (based upon particular qualities of places) and of the compelling effects of various rituals and rites performed by priests at sacred places (Sax 1991).

CHAPTER FIVE

Gaya: The Sacred City Of Ghosts Cape

Eulogized as the most sacred place for ancestral rituals, the city of Gaya and its surrounding area claims continuity of tradition at least since the eighth century CE as recounted in the Vayu Purana. The ancient writ mentions 324 holy sites related to ancestral rites, of which 84 are presently identifiable and are concentrated in the vicinity of 9 sacred centers.

At present religious travelers most typically visit only 45 of these sites, although three-quarters of the travelers perform their ancestral rites at only three places: Phalgu River, Vishnupad, and its other associated sacred centres. The cosmogony hierarchy is marked by three territorial layers: Gaya Mandala, Gaya Kshetra and Gaya Puri, within which there is a complex interweaving of themes of birth, fertility, sun and death. In the symbolic realm of the cosmic triad, Vishnu's footprints in the Vishnupad temple serve as the axis mundi, and the cardinal and solstitial points are marked by hills and other sites of the mandala.

The first clear indication of Gaya as a holy place is metaphorically eulogized in the Rig Veda (1.22.17). The treatise Nirukta, around the eighth century BCE, explains the three most sacred places in Gaya. The glory of Gaya had already been accepted in the period of the Mahabharata, especially for ancestral rites. According to inscriptional sources, the antiquity of the site and tradition of ancestral rites in and around the Vishnupad temple goes back to the period of Samudragupta (fifth century CE).

The Chinese traveler Hsuan-tsang (seventh century) also mentioned Gaya as a sacred place for bathing, which possesses the power to wash away sins. The name Gaya is derived from a demon-king, Gayasura, who by his arduous austerity, pleased the gods and was blessed that the spirit of all divinities would reside in his body. By the power he gained through deep meditation, the divine spirit met the earth spirit, resulting in the formation of a very powerful matrix. It was this fame that attracted the Buddha to come and perform meditation here. Queen Ahilyabai Holkar of Indore made major sculptural and architectural renovations in Vishnupad temple and other temples in the late eighteenth century.

The three primal objects of nature symbolism described and given ritual connotations are the Phalgu River ('flowing water'), Akshayavata ('the imperishable Banyan') and Pretashila ('the hill of the ghosts'). The river symbolizes fertility by its liquidity ('living water') in which life, strength and eternity are contained. The most common ritual period is the seven-day week (not all weeks have seven days), each day of which is prescribed for particular rituals and ancestral rites, combining scarcity with space, time and function.

The texts and traditions of Hinduism persuade devotees to perform ancestral rites at Gaya to help the spirits who, owing to karma or an untimely death, have not yet settled down. By doing this, one's forebears can finally achieve a seat in the prescribed abode of manes. This is one of the ideals of Hindus, pursued by the masses, especially in the countryside. As ancestral rites are performed, the spirits of believers' forebears are released from ghost life, which is riddled with suffering, and they are liberated from endless wandering (moksha). Each year more than a million Hindus visit Gaya to perform ancestral rites.

CHAPTER SIX

ISLAMIC PILGRIMAGE

> “ *"There is a polish for everything that takes away rust; and the polish for the heart is the remembrance of Allah." - Sahih al-Bukhari.* ”

Ajmer Sharif in Rajasthan Islam, the term means 'submission to the will of God' and the religion means 'peace, mercy, forgiveness and faith in one God who is above all, who is eternal'. Being the second largest spread religion, Islam is all about having faith in one God and his several messengers (prophets), who spread the words of the almighty. These words carry the whole essence of the beautiful world gifted by the God, by; Allah, along with the preaching on how the mankind should lead its life. Further, those divine human souls who selflessly believe and practice the Islamic religion are known as Muslims.

The Five Pillars of Islam

- **Shahadah**: reciting the Muslim profession of faith from the bottom of the heart.

- **Salat**: reciting the prayers five times each day.
- **Zakat**: doing charity for helping the poor and the needy.
- **Sawm**: fasting during the month of Ramadan.
- **Hajj**: pilgrimage to Mecca at least once in a lifetime.

These pillars are basically the most important Muslim practices that draw the ground of the respective religion and these practices are a must for every Islamic follower.

A very important prophet who not just brought the message of the God, but actually gave birth to the religion 'Islam' was "Prophet Muhammad". Complete name Abu al-Qasim Muhammad ibn 'Abd Allah ibn 'Abd al-Muttalib ibn Hashim, Prophet Muhammad was a man among the men. He was born in 570 at Mecca, Saudi Arabia and it is his life and deeds that defined Islam.

In Muslims, if there is any perfect ethical character, it is a Muhammadan character. He was very close to economically poor people and did everything that he could help them out. Further, he led a very simple life, which was completely devoted to serving the human race and worshiping Allah. Though Prophet Muhammad founded Islam, he was not the only messenger of God; there were many more.

As per Quran (the holy book of Muslims) Hazrat Adam Alaihis Salam, Hazrat Nooh Alaihis Salam, Hazrat Ibrahim Alaihis Salam, Jacob, Hazrat Musa Alaihis Salam and Hazrat Isa Alaihis Salam and his apostles, all were Muslim prophets. The reason why these men (irrespective of their different religions) are regarded as God's holy Muslim messengers is because they devoted their entire life just to spreading the teachings of the almighty, and even their deeds included the nitty-gritty of the five pillars of Islam (like praying, charity, fasting, and pilgrimage).

India is home to some of the finest mosques and holiest Dargahs. In a country where Islam is the second largest religion, India is indeed a place where this great religion has not only flourished but has also been immensely respected and adored. From the northern to the southern parts of the country, followers of Islam can find a number of holy places to bow down or even prostrate.

List of some important Islamic pilgrimage centers in India:

Jama Masjid, Delhi.

Jama Masjid, the largest mosque in India, must visit places for Muslims. Emperor Shah Jahan built the sacred mosque in 1650 with the aid of 5000 workers over a period of six years. The mosque was designed by Ustad Khalil, who was known to be the great sculptor of his time and, apart from its pious ambiance, is also known for its architectural grandeur. The carvings made in the mosque are exceptional, and the major highlight here is that none of the domes are of a similar height; each dome is different from the other. It is said that it was customary for the emperor and his courtiers to visit the mosque every Friday for attending 'Jumme ki Namaz,' the congressional prayer. Indeed, it is one of the most significant holy places of Islam in India.

Dargah Qutub Sahib, Delhi.

Reckoned to be the largest mosque in India, Jama Masjid is amongst the top must visit places for Muslims in India. The sacred mosque was built by the Emperor Shah Jahan in the year 1650 with the aid of 5000 workers over the period of 6 years. The mosque has been designed by Ustad Khalil, who was known to be the great sculptor of his time and apart from its pious ambiance is also known for its architectural grandeur. The carvings made in the mosque is exceptional and the major highlight here is that none of the domes are of similar height; each dome is different from the other. It is said that it was customary for the emperor and his courtiers to visit the mosque every Friday for attending 'Jumme ki Namaz', the congressional prayer. It is indeed one of the most significant holy places of Islam in India.

Dargah Qutub Sahib, Delhi.

Another place that seems significant for Muslims in Delhi is the Dargah Qutub Sahib. Situated near Gandak ki Baoli in the Mehrauli village, some 400 meters away from the Adham Khan's tomb, Dargah of Hazrat Qutbuddin Bakhtiyar Kaki holds high regards for people of Islam religion. Hazrat Qutubudddin was the disciple and spiritual successor of Hazrat Khwaja Moinuddin Chishti of Ajmer. It is believed that several high esteem rulers like Bahadur Shah I, Shah Alam II and Akbar II lie buried in the various enclosures around the saint's grave. It is also believed that one, who truly believes in the saint, makes a wish by tying a thread near the grave.

Hazrat Nizamuddin Dargah, Delhi.

Located amid a chaotic market area, Hazrat Nizamuddin Dargah is one of the most prominent places for Muslims to visit in India. The marble shrine of the Sufi Saint Hazrat Nizam-ud-din Auliya is a notable pilgrimage of Muslims. Other tombs in the compound include that of Jahanara (daughter of Shah Jahan) and the renowned Urdu poet Amir Khusru. The Dargah is one of the most extraordinary places to listen to Sufi music and qawwali (Islamic devotional singing) at sunset. Every Thursday, people gather here to be part of this heavenly experience. Scattered around the surrounding alleyways are more tombs, huge baoli, or step-wells.

Hazratbal Shrine, Srinagar.

Situated on the western shores of Dal Lake in Srinagar, Hazratbal Shrine is the most important Islamic site in Kashmir. The main significance of the Hazratbal Shrine lies in the fact that it houses a strand of the hair of the Prophet Mohammad, and it is the main reason why the Dargah is counted in most religious places for Muslims in India. Done in white marble dates back to the 17th century and has since been the center of attraction in the Kashmir region.

Ajmer Sharif, Rajasthan.

Accepted to be the most popular place of Islam in India, Ajmer Sharif Dargah in Rajasthan is indeed a religious destination that no Muslim should miss. It is said that no prayer at this Dargah ever goes unanswered, which is why one can see the place crowded all through the year. People of all religions are welcomed. The shrine is the resting place of the Gharib Nawaz Hazrat Khwaja Moinuddin Chisti and is the oldest and largest Dargah in South Asia.

Sheikh Salim Chishti Dargah, Fatehpur Sikri, Uttar Pradesh.

Adorned with white marble, the tomb of Hazrat Sheikh Salim Chishti occupies a prominent position among the sacred places of Islam in India. Built by Mughal Emperor Akbar, it is situated in the imperial complex of Fatehpur Sikri. Hazrat Sheikh Salim Chishti predicted that the Akbar would father three sons and the prediction came true, and Akbar's son Jahangir was named as Salim after the saint, and raised by the Sufi holy man. Mughal Emperor Akbar commissioned Dargah to honor the great saint. Every Thursday, thousands of locals visit the shrine to offer prayers to the great saint. The whole atmosphere in and around the Dargah looked divine with hundreds of men and women gathered here for the prayers. Pilgrims who pray in Dargah also offer flowers (rose) on the tomb.

Char Minar, Hyderabad.

Charminar in Hyderabad is among the most prominent heritage buildings in India. However, this monument is also significant for Muslims, as the structure was created to represent the first four caliphs of Islam. The legend shows that the monument was constructed after the prayers of Sultan Muhammad Quli Qutb Shah were completed regarding the suppression of the plague. Built from granite, mortar, and lime, this sacred structure reflects an unusual mixture of mosques and arc architecture.

Haji Ali, Mumbai.

Known for its special location on an islet in Southern Mumbai, Dargah Haji Ali is a must visit for all Muslims visiting India. Dedicated to Muslim Saint Pir Hazrat Haji Ali Shah Bukhari, the shrine is visited by thousands of pilgrims irrespective of their religion. According to a record, more than 40,000 pilgrims visit this shrine to offer Chaddar and sincere prayers. During URS (Death anniversary of the saint) and Eid-E-Milad-un-Nabi, special Islamic rituals are performed. Hazrat Haji Ali Saint is known to have given up all his worldly possessions and went to Mecca. His selfless acts towards people, making him a highly revered personality. It is also believed that he asked his followers to cast his body in a coffin in the Arabian Sea when he died. Soon after his demise, his followers did as they were asked. However, it is said that the coffin stuck on the piles of rocks, and this is where his Dargah stands today.

Cheraman Juma Mosque, Thrissur, Kerala.

Probably the oldest mosque in the country, the Cheraman Juma Masjid is said to have been built in 629 AD and then was rebuilt in the 11th century AD. The mosque takes one back in the glorious years of Islam in India and, of course, helps in achieving inner peace and tranquility. It was built on a place rewarded by the last Chera ruler who upon witnessing a miraculous phenomenon, travelled to Mecca and adopted Islam. The mosque is built in a distinctive meld of Dutch-Kerala and Hindu architectural styles.

Piran Kaliyar Sharif, Haridwar, Uttarakhand.

Piran Kaliyar, also known as Kaliyar Sharif is dedicated to Sufi Saint Hazrat Alauddin Ali Ahmed Sabir also known as Sabir Kaliyari who lies here in peace. The 13th century saint was the successor of the great Sufi poet and Saint Hazrat Baba Farid of the Chishti order. The tomb was built by Ibrahim Lodhi and typified Islamic architecture with its carved grillwork. During May–June, a 15-day Urs is celebrated at the Dargah, on which people belonging to all religions, castes, and creeds turn in multitudes. After the initial religious rituals, the Urs take on a festive mood, with quawwalis and mushairas becoming the order of the day.

Shah-e-Aalam, Ahmedabad, Gujarat.

Shah-e-Alam's Tomb also known as Rasulabad Dargah or Shah Alam no Rojo is a medieval mosque and tomb complex (Roza) in Shah Alam area of Ahmedabad. Shah-e-Alam is believed to be the son of Sayyid Burhanuddin Qutub-ul-Alam and the great grandson of the much celebrated Sayyid Jalauddin Hussain Bukhari of Uch who is also known as Makhdoom Jahaniyan Jahangasht. Shah-e-Alam was the guide of Mahmud Begada's youth, and afterwards one of the most revered of Muslim religious teachers of Ahmedabad. Therefore, it is a good idea to visit the tomb of Shah-e-Alam whose auro can still be felt in this holy Dargah.

Haji Pir Dargah, Kutch, Gujarat.

Haji Pir Dargah of Kutch is an important attraction in Gujarat Tourism; thus, it is indeed a significant place for Muslims to see in India as well. People of all religions come here to seek the blessing of Pir Haji Ali Akbar, who used to save the cows that were driven away by the local goons and dacoits in the village called Nara. He later on was entitled to be a "Haji" after his visit to the greatest pilgrimage of the followers of the Islam faith, the Haj. The locals were also used to call him Haji Pir and Zinda Pir. People here believe that those who visit the Haji Pir Dargah and make a wish never go unfulfilled. Believers also travel four miles to the Karol Pir after visiting this Dargah.

Nakhoda Mosque, Kolkata.

Reckoned to be the largest mosque in Kolkata, Nakhoda Mosque is a must see in India. Situated in the Chitpur area of the Burrabazar business district in Central Kolkata, at the intersection of Zakariya Street and Rabindra Sarani, this gigantic mosque has the capacity to accommodate around 10,000 people at a time. Abdar Rahim Osman in the year 1926 laid the foundation stone of the mosque. The architecture is based on Indo-Saracenic designing and contains a spacious prayer hall, a dome and two minarets. The entrance of the shrine has been designed like the Buland Darwaza at Fatehpur Sikri.

Pazhayangadi Mosque, Malappuram District, Kerala.

Pazhayangadi Mosque or Kondotty mosque is a 500 year-old Muslim shrine in India. It is situated in northern Kerala and is considered to be the prominent pilgrim center of Muslims in Kerala. This mosque is connected to the Muslim Saint Hazrat Muhammed Shah, also known as Kondotty Thangal. The 'Valia Nercha' fair at this mosque is celebrated for three days in February-March and is a significant festival which draws a lot of devotees from around the country.

Rauza Sharif of Sheikh Ahmed Farooqi, Sirhind-Bassi Pathana Road, Punjab.

The magnificent Rauza Sharif is a mausoleum that commemorates the burial place of Mujadid-alf-Saani Sheikh Ahmed Farooqi, Kabuli, and Sirhindi, who lived during Akbar and Jahangir (1563–1634). It is an old mosque adorned with a beautiful and spacious mausoleum that is venerated as a second Mecca by Suni Muslims. Thousands of Naqshbandi Muslims from Pakistan, Afghanistan, Indonesia, and India visit the tomb annually in or about August.

Solah Khamba Masjid, Bidar, Karnataka.

Solah Khamba Masjid or the Zenani Masjid or the sixteen-columned prayer hall was built in 1423 AD by Prince Muhammad prior to the shifting of the capital to Bidar by the Bahamanis. It is believed to be the oldest Muslim building in Bidar and is among the largest in India. Therefore, it is necessary for Muslims to learn about Islamic architecture and history. It is also said that Aurangzeb, after the conquest of Bidar, held prayers here to decree Mughal sovereignty. The steps lead to the top of a panoramic view of the countryside.

Taj-ul-Masjid, Bhopal, Madhya Pradesh.

One of the most impressive structures in Bhopal is the Taj-ul-Masjid. It is also one of the largest and most elegant Muslim mosques in India. Literally translated as 'The Crown of Mosques' could never be completed due to lack of money, and after a long lay-off, construction was resumed in 1971. The pink façade of the mosque is topped by two huge white-domed minarets pointing upwards to the sky. The mosque also has three huge bulbous domes; an impressive main hallway with attractive pillars; marble flooring and a spacious courtyard. Taj-ul-Masjid is one of the largest mosques in Asia with a large tank in the centre and an imposing double storied gateway with 4 recessed archways and 9 imposing cusped multifold openings in the main prayer hall. Some of the main features of this great mosque are the 18 story high-octagonal minars, onion-shaped marble dooms, and the gossamer fine screens of trellis working in the prayer hall.

Khwaza Bande Nawaz, Gulbarga, Karnataka.

One of the most significant monuments in Gulbarga, Karnataka, is the Khwaza Bande Nawaz Dargah. The tomb of the great Sufi saint, Khwaza Syed Mohammad Gesu Daraz, also known as Khwaza Bande Nawaz. It is a magnificent building in the Indo-Saracenic style that reflects the highlights of both cultures. The arches are in Bahmani architecture, while the paintings on the walls and domes are Turkish and Iranian in style. The Dargah is the venue of an annual 'Urs', which is attended by thousands of people irrespective of any religion. There is also an in-house library on the premises of the Dargah, where as many as 10000 books in Urdu, Persian, and Arabic on subjects ranging from history and literature are kept.

CHAPTER SEVEN

Christian Pilgrimage and Religious Places in India

India is a country with an amazing history & unmatchable heritage. The country also has a large population of Christians and has a rich history of Christian pilgrimage and religious places.

From north to south and east to west there are various Christian pilgrimages situated in India where people from all over India and also around the globe mark their presence at these various pilgrimages.

Major Christian Pilgrimage and Religious places in India:

1) Velankanni Church, Tamil Nadu:

The Church of Our Lady of Vailankanni is located in Vailankanni, a Christian pilgrimage site, 5 kilometres south of Nagapattinam. It's said that "our lady" picked Vailankanni to give the world her miracles. The Velankanni Church also referred to as the "Lourdes of the East," is one of the most renowned pilgrimages for Catholics in India. When Mother Mary, holding the infant Jesus, is said to have appeared in this tiny community in the 16th or 17th century, that is when the church's history began. Christian pilgrims travel to Vailankanni from all over the world, particularly from Malaysia and Sri Lanka.

2) The Basilica of Bom Jesus, Goa:

A must-visit church in India is the magnificent church of Bom Jesus, which is famous for housing St. Francis Xavier's tomb. The church is the richest in Goa since it is encased in marble & inlaid with priceless stones. St. Francis Xavier's mortal remains are stored in a basilica with baroque-style architecture. The body of St. Francis is enclosed in a silver casket and is placed within a glass coffin. One of the most well-known Christian pilgrimage sites in India, which attracts a huge number of people every year. The first minor basilica in India, this Jesuit church is regarded as one of the finest specimens of baroque & Portuguese Colonial architecture in the country. It belongs to the list of the seven world wonders of Portuguese heritage.

3) Santa Cruz Basilica, Fort Kochi, Kerala:

One of the eight basilicas in India is the Santa Cruz Cathedral Basilica in Fort Kochi. This Keralan landmark is also one of the most magnificent churches in all of India. This basilica, the cathedral church of the Diocese of Cochin, the second-oldest Diocese in India, is next to the well-known St. Francis Church. With the advent of Portuguese missionaries in 1500 CE, the Santa Cruz Cathedral Basilica's history began in the sixteenth century. When the Cochin Raja granted the first Portuguese Viceroy Dom Francisco de Almeida permission to construct a church, construction work began. Due to its unparalleled grandeur and beauty, the cathedral has become a must-visit location in Fort Kochi.

4) St. Thomas Cathedral Basilica, Tamil Nadu:

One of the 12 Apostles of Jesus Christ, St. Thomas, was given the responsibility of spreading the Lord's teachings and Santhome Basilica is a revered shrine that is devoted to him. It is one of the most well-liked pilgrimage tourist attractions in Chennai. It is also known as St. Thomas Cathedral Basilica of the International Shrine of St. Thomas. This modest Roman Catholic Basilica was constructed in honor of the Patron Saint of India. The Catholic Bishops' Conference of India declared it a national shrine. It serves as the focal point of the Madras & Mylapore Roman Catholic Archdiocese. It is one of only three buildings from the apostolic era of early Christianity that are still intact today and are notable for housing an apostle's tomb. The other two are St. Peter's Basilica in Vatican City & Santiago de Compostela Cathedral in Galicia, Spain.

5) St. Andrew's Basilica, Kerala:

In Kerala's Alappuzha district, Arthunkal is a significant destination for Christian pilgrims. The feast of St. Sebastian has made Arthunkal famous, despite the Church's bearing the name of St. Andrew the Apostle. Before the 7th century, Christians are believed to have resided in Arthunkal, and

Jesuit missionaries began their work there in 1530 after the Portuguese visited Kerala. Christians and missionaries fought tooth and nail from 1560 until the Muthedath king eventually granted permission in 1581 for the construction of the Church. St Andrews was finally constructed using coconut palm leaves & wood on November 30th.

6. Se Cathedral Church, Goa

The Cathedral stands to the west of the great square called Terreiro de Sabaio and has its façade turned to the east. It's beautiful courtyard is approached by a flight of steps. The building is Portuguese-Gothic in style with a Tuscan exterior and Corinthian interior. The church is 250 ft in length and 181 ft in breath. The frontispiece stands 115 ft high.

7. Christ Church, Shimla

Christ Church, which is situated in the centre of the town of Shimla is believed to be the second oldest church in North India. This sacred church is the prominent landmark of Shimla that reflects the beauty of British era architecture. Built in the Neo-Gothic style in 1857, the church contains five fine stained glass windows and each window represents different Christian virtues of Faith, Hope, Charity, Fortitude, Patience and Humility.

8. Medak Cathedral, Telangana, Hyderabad

Medak Cathedral is the seat of the Bishop in Medak for the Church of South India. It was consecrated on 25 December 1924. Built by the British Wesleyan Methodists, the Cathedral is now under the jurisdiction of the Church of South India. The Cathedral is the largest of all churches in Andhra Pradesh. The Cathedral also sees over the Diocese of Medak, which is the single largest diocese in Asia and the second largest diocese in the world.

9. St. Paul Cathedral, Kolkata

St. Paul's Cathedral of Kolkata is recognized as the first Episcopal Church of the Eastern World. The construction of the church was initiated under the benefaction of Bishop Daniel Wilson in 1839 and was completed in 1847 St Paul's Cathedral is acknowledged as the first Episcopal Church of the eastern world. Itis an Anglican cathedral of the Church of North India. Besides, being a religious site, the cathedral is also an architectural marvel. St. Paul's Cathedral is 247 feet in length, 81 feet in width and 114 feet at transept. The flagstaff rises to a height of 175 feet above ground level.

10. Basilica of Holy Rosary Church, Hooghly, Kolkata

Basilica of Holy Rosary was established around 1660 and is one of the oldest churches in West Bengal. The Basilica of the Holy Rosary commonly known as Bandel Church is one of the oldest Christian churches in West Bengal, India. Bandel Church is a Roman Catholic Church Situated in Bandel, Hooghly district of West Bengal. On November 25, 1988, Pope John Paul II declared the sanctuary a minor basilica.

11. St. Thomas Syro-Malabar Catholic Church, Palayoor

St Thomas is an important Christian pilgrimage in Kerala. The church is named after St. Thomas, the apostle who is believed to have spread the teachings of Christianity in South India. It is among the old churches in India and dates back to 52 AD. It is also believed that church was built by St. Thomas himself, thus it has been declared as an international pilgrimage spot by the Vatican. Since it is on the hill top, climbing the hill, it offers a great experience to the worshipers to get to the church and prays.

12. St. Thomas Church, Guruvayoor

St. Thomas, the Apostle of Christ landed in AD 52 at Kodungalur, the first centaury west coast harbor of Kerala (Pliny's Primum Emporium India) and went on to establish seven churches for the faithful he evangelized in Kerala. Only one of the seven churches could claim continuous existence in the same location from the time of the Apostle. The church at Palayur is unique in that the present church has a continuous history of two millennia and stands on the same spot where Apostle first established it.

13. Parumala Church, Parumala, Kerala

Named after the great Saint, Saint Gregorious Geevarghese, Parumala is a parish church of the Malankara Orthodox Syrian Church in Thiruvalla district of Kerala. It is also known as the tomb of Saint Gregorious Geevarghese. The church can accommodate about 2000 people at a time. It is in a circular church with a diameter of 39 meters and is believed to have great miracle powers.

14. Rosary Church, Shetihalli, Hassan.

The Shettihalli Church is believed to have been built around 450 years ago and represents a Gothic architecture. The Hemavathy River backwaters submerge the church, but the water recedes during the summer time and tourists can visit the ruins of the church during this time. Prayers are held once, with lamps lighting up the church during this time. Even when the church is half under the water, tourists can go near it on a coracle.

15. Our Lady of the Immaculate Conception Church, Goa

The church has interior which is relatively simple by the standards of the time. There are two flanking altars that catch the eye, out of which one on the left is dedicated to Jesus Crucified and that on the right to Our Lady of the Rosary. This Church is located in the heart of Panjim city.

The Our Lady of the Immaculate Conception Church is one of the oldest churches in Goa, which existed from the year 1540. It is among the first churches to be built in Goa with its church bells being the second largest in the world

16. St. Anne Church, Goa

The Church of Anne was declared a national monument in 1931 during the Portuguese era as per Government Portario. The Church, located on the banks of River Siridao, was first conceived by Fr. Mons Francisco do Rego. He started the construction with his own contributions and some from the villagers around the area. It is very interesting to know that Fr. Francisco do Rego's ancestors were Hindu Brahmins from a nearby village of Neura. The construction of Church of St. Anne began in the year 1577 and was completed by 1695, long after Fr. Francisco do Rego passed away. The work of the construction was taken over by his successor, Fr. Antonio Francisco da Cunha.

17. Moravian Church, Leh

The church was first consecrated in Leh (Ladakh) by German missionaries in 1834 that brought some local Buddhist residents into their fold. Belonging to the Protestant denomination, the church has a history of being a successful attempt of missionaries to far-flung places in India.

18. All Saints Cathedral, Allahabad

All Saints Cathedral in Allahabad was built in the late 19th century and today stands remarkably as colonial structure. All Saints Cathedral Church was designed by Sir William Emerson in the year 1870. The intricate work and designs on the marble altar and the stained glass panel makes the building more attractive. The Gothic style of architecture of the All Saints Cathedral Church, Allahabad in Uttar Pradesh in India has been a major Tourist

Attraction in Allahabad.

19. St. Philomena's Church, Mysore

St. Philomena's is a Roman Catholic Church that was built in AD 1840. Earlier known as St. Joseph Chaver, the church has twin towers that stands majestically at175 feet. St. Philomena's Church in Mysore is considered to be the second largest church in Asia. This Roman Catholic Church was built to honor the memory of Saint Philomena, a Latin Catholic Saint and martyr of the Roman Catholic Church. Located in the northern part of the city, St. Philomena's Church is the most famous address on the ever-busy Ashoka Road of Mysore. The church is renowned for its spectacular architecture in the Neo Gothic style.

20. Immaculate Conception Cathedral, Puducherry

Immaculate Conception Cathedral is known as "Samba Kovil" The church bears a resemblance with church in France that was built in 1791 on the ruins of the older church. Boasting of an imposing facade with paired Doric columns below and ionic above and interior design consisting eight barrel vaults and a central dome pierced with eight circular openings, the church is a fine specimen of the French architecture in India.

21. St. Aloysius Chapel, Mangalore

Established in the year 1885, St. Aloysius Chapel bears resemblance with world's most renowned Sistine Chapel at Rome. The Aloysius Chapel is considered a world-class tourist destination, with amazing architecture, extraordinary layouts and a well though execution that matches none. Come and be at one with God and the beauty of his creation and enjoy the peace and tranquility of the atmosphere. You will go back rejuvenated and relaxed.

22. Cathedral of The Sacred Heart, Delhi

Cathedral of the Sacred Heart is popular as one of the most prestigious of Catholic Churches in Delhi. The church is situated amidst the 14 acres of lush greenery. Cathedral of the Sacred Heart in Delhi is located near Gol Dak Khana at the intersection of Ashoka Road and Baba Kharak Singh Marg. Cathedral of the Sacred Heart is popular as one of the most prestigious of Catholic Churches of the capital. History says that when the plan of building this church, was hatched, eight architects were summoned. However, the design was finally conceived by Henry Medd.

CHAPTER EIGHT

Socio-Economic Impacts in Pilgrimage Tourism

Businesses and public organizations are increasingly interested in the economic impacts of tourism at national, state, and local levels. One regularly hears claims that tourism supports X jobs in an area or that a festival or special event generated Y million dollars in sales or income in a community.

"Multiplier effects" are often cited to capture secondary effects of tourism spending and show the wide range of sectors in a community that may benefit from tourism. Tourism's economic benefits are touted by the industry for a variety of reasons. Claims of tourism's economic significance give the industry greater respect among the business community, public officials, and the public in general. This often translates into decisions or public policies that are favorable to tourism. Community support is important for tourism, as it is an activity that affects the entire community. Tourism businesses depend extensively on each other as well as on other businesses, government and residents of the local community.

Economic benefits and costs of tourism reach virtually everyone in the region in one way or another. Economic impact analyses provide tangible estimates of these economic interdependencies and a better understanding of the role and importance of tourism in a region‘s economy. Tourism activity also involves economic costs, including the direct costs incurred by tourism businesses, government costs for infrastructure to better serve tourists, as well as congestion and related costs borne by individuals in the community. Community decisions over tourism often involve debates between industry proponents touting tourism‘s economic impacts (benefits) and detractors emphasizing tourism‘s costs. Sound decisions rest on a balanced and objective assessment of both benefits and costs and an understanding of who benefits from tourism and who pays for it.

Tourism‘s economic impacts are therefore an important consideration in state, regional and community planning and economic development. Economic impacts are also important factors in marketing and management decisions. Communities therefore need to understand the relative importance of tourism to their region, including tourism‘s contribution to economic activity in the area. A variety of methods, ranging from pure guesswork to complex mathematical models, are used to estimate tourism‘s economic impacts. Studies vary extensively in quality and accuracy, as well as which aspects of tourism are included. Technical reports often are filled with economic terms and methods that non-economists do not understand.

On the other hand, media coverage of these studies tend to oversimplify and frequently misinterpret the results, leaving decision makers and the general public with a sometimes distorted and incomplete understanding of tourism's economic effects. How can the average person understand these studies sufficiently to separate good studies from bad ones and make informed choices? The purpose of this bulletin is to present a systematic introduction to economic impact concepts and methods. The presentation is written for tourism industry analysts and public officials, who would like to better understand, evaluate, or possibly conduct an economic impact assessment. The bulletin is organized around ten basic questions that either are asked or should be asked about the economic impacts of tourism.

HISTORICAL PERSPECTIVE OF RELIGIOUS TOURISM IN INDIA:

India is a land of pilgrimage. Travel for religious purposes has been there from the most ancient times. Practically, all religions – Hindu, Buddhism, Jainism and Sikhism have their major and minor pilgrimage centers in different parts of the country. There are also centers of Sufism, churches and mosques that are visited by people. In fact, to a majority of domestic tourists in India pilgrimage has always been the main motivation.

In India, all major temples, shrines and sacred spots are found scattered all along major riverbanks or in the hills. The confluence of holy rivers called 'Sangam', attract millions of tourists every year when pilgrims assemble there to take holy dip in these rivers. For example on the day of 'Sankranti' a bath in holy Ganga water is believed to relieve a person of all the sins.

Another dimension added to it is that an effort to unify the country Adi Shankaracharya established four peeth (centres) in the four corners of the country. They are Badrinath in North, Kanchipuram in South, Dwarkapuri in West and Jagannath Puri in East. To add to this Sringerimutt in Karnataka state is also claimed to be the sacred peeth.

The Indian pilgrims travel to the holy temples, the Indian holy space called 'Teerth' which contain the meaning of 'to cross'. It is a clear indication that in Indian holy space something is being crossed over. Within the holy space human beings are given the chance to transcend themselves when they come face to face, in contemplation, with the divinity. The pilgrimage, instead of diminishing in our apparently ever more secular, scientific and technologically oriented world, is experiencing considerable growth. This is primarily because in religious life of an average Indian, even rivers have played a decisive role.

The rivers from time immemorial have been the symbol of purity to humans. Among these rivers the Ganga is believed to be the most sacred for all Hindus. Innumerable holy shrines like Gaumukh, Gangotri, Devprayag, Rishikesh, Hardwar, Garmukteshwar, Kannauj, Allahabad, Varanasi, Patna and Gangasagar have come up on her banks through ages. These holy shrines attract millions of domestic pilgrims every year. On the other hand, river Yamuna is considered to be most meritorious to perform Gayatri Jap, worship of Keshav, Shiv or the Sun. The month of 'Kartik' is pious for taking bath in Yamuna at Mathura. Traditions believe that Godavari before dividing itself into seven branches and meeting the sea, is most sacred for bath referred to as 'Sapta Sagar Yatra'.

Besides rivers, sacred shrines have been visited extensively by domestic tourists all along the periods. The twelve Jyotirlingas, five Bhutalingas and many other temples enshrining 'Lingas' in their sanctorum are the ideal terminal destinations of domestic tourists since the time of great epics. The Jyotirlingas are at Kedarmath (Uttaranchal), Kashi Vishwanath (Uttar Pradesh), Somnath (Gujarat), Baijnath (Karnataka), Rameshwaram (Tamil Nadu), Ghushneshwar (Maharashtra), Bhimashankar (Maharashtra), Mahakaleshwar (Madhya Pradesh), Mallikarjuna (Andhra Pradesh), Omkareshwar (Madhya Pradesh), Nageshwar (Gujarat) and Tryambakeshwar (Maharashtra). The Bhutalingas are at Kalahastishwar (Vayulinga) at Kalahasti; Jambukeshwar (Appulinga) at Trichy; Arunachaleshwar (Bhatalinga) at Thriuvannamalai; Ekambareshwar (Prithvilinga) at Kanchipuram and Chidambareshwar (Akaslinga) at Chidambaram.

In addition to also holy rivers and sacred shrines situated on the banks of these rivers, 'Shakti' is also worshipped as the Divine mother, a creative power both as an enforcing discipline and for securing righteousness. There are nearly fifty-one shakti peethas all over the country. These peethas are visited by tourists throughout the year. Thus, the religious tourism is a mixture of both ancient and modern cultures, i.e., from the exodus of the past to the present day where religious tourism has become a mainstay of tourism.

India is a country abounding in not only Hindu shrines but she also represents manifestations of elevating and inspiring works of Jain Tirthankars at Sravasti, Kaushambi, Hastinapur, Parasnath hills, Rajgiris, Khandgiri, Udaigiri, Khajuraho and Dilwara Temples at Mount Abu. Islami (Sufis) shrines as centres of religious influence at Ajmer

(Khwaja Moinuddin Chisti), Gulbarga (Khwaja Bande Nawaj); Faridkot; Delhi (Sheikh Nizammudin Aulia); and Panipat (Shah Sharaf Bin Ali). Sikh religion though believed that real pilgrimage is inward yet their sacred shrines are located at Garhwal (Hemkund Sahib); Amritsar (Golden Temple); Taran Taaran (Anandpur Sahib), Kartarpur and Patna Sahib; Churches in Goa. At many of these centers festivals and fairs are also held.

Socio-Economic Impacts in Pilgrimage Tourism:

Most studies that measured specifically the impacts of pilgrimage tourism agree that sacred destinations are strongly affected by the stream of pilgrimage tourists visiting them (CollinsKreiner et al., 2006; Rinschede, 1992; Vukonic, 1996; Din, 1989; Walpole and Goodwin,2000). Shinde (2003) proposes a model of the dynamics of pilgrimage tourism, which allows us to further understand the interaction between pilgrimage tourists and host community and the associated impacts. As depicted there is both an immediate impact on the hosts' environment due to the direct contact of the visitors with the religious institutions, and also an indirect impact on the local economy and the society.

First and most obvious impact of pilgrimage tourism is through the visits to the religious site and the visitor's contact with the religious institutions. However, apart from the religious institutions, holy sites are often surrounded by religiously orientated businesses and facilities, such as souvenir shops, travel agencies, hotels and even hospitals, providing employment for the host community (Evans, 1998). In particular, the sale of religious souvenir items, for example sacred water (Maseeh, 2002), icons and candles (Evans, 1998) or other religious things (Dubish, 1995) brings in considerable revenue, as is the case in Assisi in

Italy and Lourdes in France (Fleischer, 2000).According to Secall (2003), this material perspective of interest brought about by pilgrimages has always been present in human history.

As such, religious tourism can have similar economic impact as we see in other forms of tourism such as job creation, population growth and infrastructure development. The Catholic pilgrimage site Lourdes is a good example of how pilgrimage tourism can affect a destination's population growth. Lourdes, which currently receives some 6 million pilgrims per year from 140 different countries, (Lourdes, 2007) has been experiencing a constant population growth since its beginning as a pilgrimage site in 1858. This is in contrast to other cities at the edge of the Pyrenees and is attributable to the arrival of people from the surrounding area for job opportunities provided by the pilgrimage (Rinschede, 1992). Czestochowa in Poland, a town with a population of 250,000 attracts some 4.5 million pilgrims per year (Czestochowa, 2008; Gray, 2008) saw improving its infrastructure as a result of being a pilgrimage site (Jackowski and Smith, 1992).

Some religious sites have been visited for centuries and there the impacts develop over a long period of time but sometimes holy sites are discovered suddenly, bringing dramatic and sudden changes to the local residents. Medjugorje in Bosnia-Herzegovina is one such example. Vukonic (1992, 1996, 2002) explains how the discovery of a holy shrine in 1981 resulted in a sudden growth of private accommodation and in land price inflation.

In the Islamic world, income generated from the pilgrims to Mecca is the second major pillar of Saudi Arabian economy after oil (Aktas and Ekin, 2007).

Pilgrimage generates annual revenues of approximately $8 billion and over the past 30 years Saudi Arabiahas invested $35 billion in improving facilities for pilgrims (Salih, 2003). Pilgrimage tourism is of course not free from negative impacts. El-Bakry (2003) notes that the high cost of an umra or hajj trip for Muslim people plus the increase in the number of people performing umra, gave rise to a black market for the exchange rate of the Saudi riyal. More precisely, the Saudi riyal increased 16% between Novembers.

Role of Religious Tourism in Balance Economic Growth:

In India, religious tourism plays a vital role in narrowing economic imbalance. Most of the places, especially rural areas and the areas which have no core competence or business, survive due to religious tourism. It provides business and employment opportunities to local population helps to take care of their requirements. For instance, 'Sulli Karadu' a small dry rural area near Coimbatore, Tamil Nadu, India, well known for a rural deity which is very powerful, ought to be worshipped by offering Camphor in big quantities which is available in nearby shops. Devotees stand in mile long queue to offer their offerings. It provides livelihood to local population who sell camphor to the devotees which is supplied by camphor manufacturers.

Also, it was interpreted that the whole exercise was orchestrated by the camphor manufacturers to sell their products which has been banned by Tamil Nadu Endowment Board to camphor in temples, by quoting the reason that would spoil the environment. However, this is a classical example on the religious tourism which fed the whole village. Also, a place called "Thadi Kombu" near Madurai, well known for a deity viz. "Shorna Bairavar" which is very powerful to collect the bad debts, it is the believe that if a pilgrim visit the place for 8 times in a particular day of the month, his/her prayers would be answered. This generates employment opportunities in the sleeping semi-urban small town, also generated business for bus owners who take devotees for charter trips on that particular day from far off places.

These are all the examples of small places which generates business and employment opportunities for the local population, let alone, many famous places like "Palani", Madurai, Rameswaram, Kanyakumar, etc. in Tamil Nadu, and well known, "Sabari Malai" in kerala, which generates millions and provides employment opportunities to many. The whole kerala belt has been benefiting from lakhs for devotees visit sabari malai during particular seasons. These provide tremendous opportunities for marketers to focus on these locations to market their products and services. It is the dual benefit of catering location population as well to promote the products/ services.

Strategies to Enhance Religious Tourism through Corporate Market Responsibility (CRP):

Definitely, the marketers would get benefit out of the booming religious tourism as they could find new territories to sell their products and services. They would also take part in developing these Places along with local development authorities.

a) Marketers could participate in providing basic sanitary facilities along with they could promote their products viz. If X company sponsors the Free or Paid Rest room facilities, its products would only be sold.

b) Marketers could also participate in constructing rooms for devotees to stay and promote their products

c) Marketers could offer free/paid transportation facilities which will carry the promotion of their products/ services

d) Pharmaceutical companies could sponsor free medical camps in which their products could be promoted

e) Food products companies could set up their outlets to sell products with subsidized /actual prices

f) Clothing/Garment companies could set up their stalls to promote their products and services.

It clearly shows that there is enough room for marketers to participate in Corporate Market Responsibility which offers the dual benefit of offering services to the society as well to promote their products/services. This would definitely provide a lucrative mind space in potential target group in which would not have done by spending millions on conventional promotion tools. Hence, it is the marketers and the state and central government could join their hands to concentrate on these locations in order to generate business and employment opportunities as well to promote their products/services.

If this done, the government would not worry about offering minimum 100 days employment opportunities, they will take care of themselves. The government could seek help from marketers to offer necessary infrastructure support viz. transportation, water and sanitation, power and other basic facilities which ensure the influx and pleasant stay of pilgrims.

RELIGIOUS TOURISM – UNITING THE NATION:

Religion may be a dicey word in recent Indian political lexicon, yet, unites the country from Kashmir to Kanyakumari. This article does not discuss the intricacies of religion and its role in India; it does discuss the economic face of religion in removing economic disparity across the country. Comparing the different countries across the globe, India is surprisingly possess different religions viz. Hinduism, Islam, Christianity, Buddhism, Sikhism, Jainism, Persian to name a few, yet, the people embrace different religions live together. Also, people belong to different religions visit other religions sacred locations which is very unique and surprising. India is a country of complex culture, yet people live with understanding and tolerance.

It is always an amazing place for researchers who involve in behavioral science. People belong to different religions; follow different customs, traditions, having different life style, tastes and preferences, which always pose a challenge for marketers and global companies send their global managers to India to get trained as it plays a role of potential training ground. Marketers also focus on encasing the religious believe of the population by targeting religious tourism locations to market their locations viz. Kumbamela at Varanasi, Allahabad, Rajmundry etc. are the hottest locations for the marketers to target their potential consumers. These locations woo many pilgrims across the country and provide a bouquet of potential consumers at one place which provides a platform to companies to reach the mass at nominal cost of promotion.

India possesses many pilgrimage locations across the country from north to south to east to west which bridges the economic disparity of the population. Movement of domestic tourists to different places ensures the movement of money to the required places. For instance, Tirupathi is the famous religious location in Andhra Pradesh which woos people across the country and world. It is treated the richest pilgrimage location next to Vatican. Tirupathi generates employment opportunities to many and supports considerable number of population. Considering the core competence i.e. the ability of the place to generate employment opportunities with certain skill sets of the people of Tirupathi, it contains none. Yet, with the famous Balaji Temple, it runs like a multinational company spins billions in revenues per year.

Carnival for Marketers:

Many companies target religious locations to promote their existing and new products which they find very opt to reach the target group. Even, companies sponsor religious festivals viz. Ramco, Birla, to name a few, in order to win the hearts and minds of people. Recent 'Kumbhmela in Allahabad and Rajmundry, paved a root to billions of business to local and multinational conglomerates. These places are considered special rendezvous for marketers to promote products and services with nominal cost. Most of the companies set up free food stalls, camping tents, drinking water fountains, medical treatment camps to serve the pilgrims visit the places. This is an innovative approach normally be executed to capture the hearts of potential target group. This would provide a mind space for products and services which they may consider buy these brands in future. These are the practices to create an experience and attitude about brands before the actual usage.

Income Generated within the Country:

Income in an economy can be generated from various sources like salary, wages, rent, taxes, interest, profit, and so on. The expenditure made by one person is the income of another person. Income is created directly or indirectly. Tourism, a labor intensive service industry, can create direct as well as indirect income from tourist expenditure by providing tourist goods and services. For example, expenditure in hotels, investment in infrastructure development, taxis, car parking, catering services, purchase of goods, and services like water, electricity, gas, food and beverages etc all result in income generation.

The flow of money generated by tourism multiplies many times as it passes through various sections of economy. ***This is known as the multiplier effect of tourism earnings***. It is the extra income produced in an economy as a result of the initial spending of money. This extra income is again invested directly or indirectly and there can be different rounds of income generation. Along with the initial spending and with each round of spending of tourism income, some benefits of spending may be dissipated through different sources known as leakages.

Savings made by individuals or by the country, tourists purchasing imported goods, imports to be made by the local people, remittances of income outside the country etc are the examples of leakages. There is an inverse relation between tourism income multiplier and proportion of leakages. As the proportion of leakage is high, the proportion of tourism income is low and vice versa. Money spent by tourists (tourist expenditure) does not stop moving after it is spent; rather it circulates through the economy of the country. When a tourist visits a place and spends his money in that particular region, part of this money becomes income for the people living in that region. Part of this income is spent which generates income for others to spend. A part of this income is again spent and so on and so forth. This money changes hands a number of times and is spent and re-spent. This impact of this expenditure on the nation's economy will go on multiplying if it is spent and changes hands again and again. Thus the national currency exchanged for foreign currency that enters the country spreads quickly in the market.

The intensity of the multiplier depends on the proportion of the income from tourism that is redistributed to other branches of the national economy. The Master Plan of 1986 of the Government of Kerala says: —tourism Industry looms large in the economic sphere of Kerala as a potential revolutionary agent of change. A well-organized thrust in the field of tourism can attract millions of people to Kerala from other parts of India and abroad and ensure a steady flow of vast sums to the state demanding a variety of services and goods and thereby providing employment to an ever-increasing number people, educated and uneducated. In fact there is no other industry which can meet successfully some of the most vexed problems of Kerala such as poverty and unemployment.

The tourist expenditure has a tremendous effect on the economy of the host country. From the frontline level it diffuses into the inner levels of the economy. The direct effect or the first round effect is the most obvious effect of tourism spending. The effect is created in the front-line tourist sectors of provisioning of tourist goods and services. Expenditures on hotels, restaurants, taxies, railways, domestic airlines, tourism generated exports etc are included in this group. The direct impact is in general and depends on the capability of the destination to provide for tourist demands. The indirect effect is a series of the successive rounds of secondary expenditure by suppliers to the tourist sectors, which results from the direct expenditure. Purchase of goods and services by the front-line establishments from local suppliers and wholesalers and from other sections within the local economy constitute indirect effect. Generally, indirect effect will be less than the direct effect because of the leakages in the direct effect. The incremental local incomes accrued to the local people in the form of direct or indirect income may be spent or re spent for non-tourism goods and services. Such income generates further additional rounds of income and it is called induced effect of tourist income. For example, hotel workers purchasing goods and services from their wages.

Creation of job opportunities; local people are employed in different sectors of the tourism industry; opportunities for women. New fields for commercial activities; Tourism opens up new possibilities for ventures; attracts new investment in the city. Tourist spending; Tourist spending provides the necessary income for preserving and managing places of attraction. Such spending also becomes a source of revenues for municipal councils (E.G parking, tourist taxes etc).

Tourist spending are spread in different sectors and create jobs and revenues on sectors indirectly related to the tourism industry; contribution to local wealth, economic development and regeneration.

Conclusions:

The results of the foregoing study have clearly demonstrated that pilgrimage tourism is playing a major role in socio-economic development. Among other observations, it has shown that, for many countries of the region, the economic significance of pilgrimage tourism is very large when measured against GDP and exports. For many countries in general and the least developed countries in particular, pilgrimage tourism is a sector in which they have comparative, if not competitive, advantages for which they can efficiently convert domestic resources into foreign exchange. If appropriately used, such foreign exchange can purchase the investment goods necessary to support more broadly based economic development policies. . The study has demonstrated that the social significance of pilgrimage tourism, measured in terms of employment (especially unskilled labor), is very large. It has also illustrated that appropriate pilgrimage tourism-related interventions can play a role in raising the standard of living and in reducing poverty in local communities. It is often necessary, however, to develop and implement policies that take advantage of the potential benefits of pilgrimage tourism in socioeconomic development. In some cases, this is simply a matter of increasing awareness so that the joint benefits to pilgrimage tourists and local communities can be —factored-in‖ at the planning stage. In other cases it may involve reducing leakages (or retaining pilgrimage tourist spending). In yet other cases —affirmative action‖ may need to be taken to capture the benefits. In any event, there is a strong case for considering pilgrimage tourism as an important sector in socio-economic development.

Source:http://zenithresearch.org.in/images/stories/pdf/2012/Jan/ZIJMR/24%20S%20VIJAY%20ANAND%20tourism.pdf

The Author

Dr. Anshumali Pandey is a renowned & reliable name in the field of Education, Hospitality, Tourism and Tribal Food. He is a Teacher and Chef by profession, and also an Author, a Business Auditor, and an avid culinary traveller to the Indian Sub continental hinterlands. Dr. Anshumali Pandey is a Hospitality Educator (PhD) who specialises in Higher Education, Office Administration, Pay roll, HR, Labour Laws, Audit, and Procurement & Tender Process. He is an Author with 74 Publications consisting of 56 Books and 3 short stories.

His contribution and research in the field of Tribal Food, Tribal Tourism, Forest Tourism and Village Tourism in the form of research papers have brought several laurels to him. In 2018 the Ministry of Tourism, Govt of Indian duly recognised all this and awarded him with a National Appreciation certificate and memento.

The books written by **Dr Anshumali Pandey** are essentially a banquet arising from an experience of over 25 years of Professional life and have boiled down to crisp and accurate writing on his favourite subjects. Hospitality Sector champion requires to be a specialist in many fields and Dr Pandey is one of them. His knowledge is evident from the spectrum of subjects which he has chosen for his books so far, which ranges from being a specialist chef, to Master of Human resources, to Education and to love for children, and topped with Spirituality. For more than two decades Dr Pandey has lived with his family in Western India in general and the Tribal belt of the union territory of Dadra & Nagar Haveli in particular. Most of his time is consumed in helping and understanding the Tribal and rural population of the region and writing scholarly articles and books on his vast area of interest.

Books written by the Author are –

1. Theory of Indian Cookery
2. Beauty and Irony of Silvassa Tourism
3. A Short Indian Food Story
4. Be Your Own Guide to Indian Cuisine
5. Cookery Fundamentals
6. History of Indian Food (2 Editions Printed)
7. The Great Indian Story Book for Children
8. Personal Budget: Easy Work Book
9. Online Classes Log Book
10. Dictionary Making Work Book for School Children
11. The Lazy Bed
12. Hindu Dharm (हन्दि्ू धर्म) (In Hindi Language)

13. Where is my coffee?
14. Your First Job is Never your Last (Volume 1)
15. You are Almost There (Quick Fix Resume and Interview Hacks)
16. Working for the Enemy? - A lesson in Career Management
17. Public Speaking for the Young
18. A Date With Coffee
19. How to be The Best Hotel Front Office Employee
20. Diploma in Food Production, The complete Syllabus
21. Diploma in F&B Service, The Complete Syllabus
22. Diploma in Front Office, The Complete Syllabus
23. The Time to Speak is Now
24. Munshi Premchand (Short Stories in English)
25. The Housekeeping Department, Text Book
26. Hitchhiker's Guide to Trekking in Uttarakhand
27. Uttarakhand, A divine Land for a Reason
28. Bachhon ke liye rochak kahaniyan (बच्चों के लिए रोचक कहानियाँ) (In Hindi Language)
29. Basic Communication Skills of English
30. The Basic Office Organisation Book for Start-ups
31. Hospitality HRM
32. Hospitality Marketing
33. Bakery Ingredients and Tools
34. Human Resource Management for Indian Professionals
35. The process of LAWFULLY operating a Hospitality business in India
36. Indian Classical Sweets: History, Tradition and Recipes
37. History of India's Himalayan Cuisine: Classical Cookery of Kashmir, Laddakh, Jammu, Himachal, Lahaul, Spiti, Garhwal, Kumaon.
38. Vindu: Andhra Cuisine (Part 1 of South Indian Trilogy)

39. Saappadu: Tamil Cuisine (Part 2 of South Indian Trilogy)
40. Sadya: Malayali Cuisine (Part 3 of South Indian Trilogy)
41. South Indian Cuisine - The Researcher's Guide Book
42. The Ramayana for Children and other short stories from Indian Mythology
43. Legends of the Tribal Shiva
44. Third Generation Children's Story Book
45. It's Elementary: The Top Nine Adventures from the memoirs of Dr John H Watson
46. UNITY IN DIVERSITY, The foundation of Indian Tourism
47. The Thar Express: Culinary History of Rajasthan and Gujarat
48. Basics of Computerized Accounting
49. Impact (Impact of Globalization on Indian Social Life)
50. Vishnu – The Lord of Amazing Incarnations
51. Being a Mahatma in the Freedom Struggle
52. The Culinary Journey of Purvanchal: Lucknow to Patna
53. Culinary History of the Gangetic Plains
54. Indian Culinary Secrets
55. The Story of Jain and Parsi Food
56. The Great Indian Pilgrimage Tourism

Connect with me: anshumali.pandey@gmail.com
https://notionpress.com/author/337004

Please scan this QR code on your phone to know more about the latest and complete works of Dr Anshumali Pandey

9 798889 514299

Printed by Libri Plureos GmbH in Hamburg,
Germany